A
gift
honoring
Griffin
and
Carson
Gilchrist

A History of Pirates

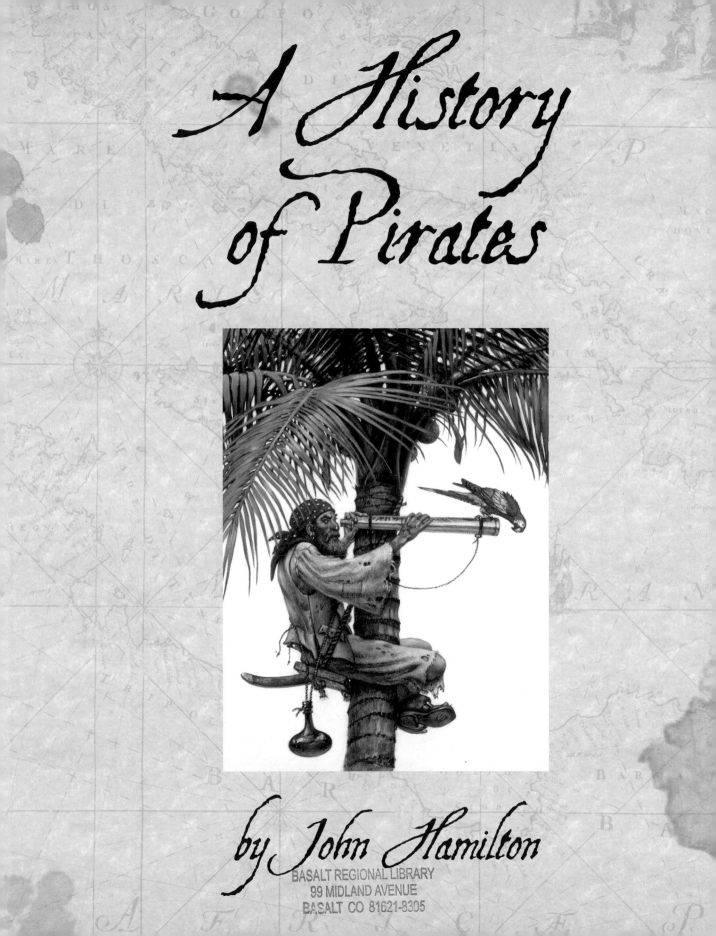

by John Hamilton

Visit us at
www.abdopublishing.com

Published by ABDO Publishing Company, 4940 Viking Drive, Suite 622, Edina, Minnesota 55435.
Copyright ©2007 by Abdo Consulting Group, Inc. International copyrights reserved in all countries.
No part of this book may be reproduced in any form without written permission from the publisher.
ABDO & Daughters™ is a trademark and logo of ABDO Publishing Company.

Printed in the United States.

Editors: Sue Hamilton/Tad Bornhoft
Graphic Design: John Hamilton
Cover Design: Neil Klinepier
Cover Illustration: *No Prey, No Pay*, ©1993 Don Maitz
Interior Photos and Illustrations: p 1 *Bird's Eye View*, ©1996 Don Maitz; p 3 *Dead Men Tell No Tales*, ©2003 Don Maitz; p 5 *No Prey, No Pay*, ©1993 Don Maitz; p 6 satellite view of Strait of Hormuz, NASA; p 7 (upper right) Viking raiders, Corbis; p 7 (bottom) map of Mediterranean Sea, Mariners' Museum; p 8 *Bird's Eye View*, ©1996 Don Maitz; p 9 Spanish frigate, Mary Evans Picture Library; p 11 map of Spanish Main, Mariners' Museum; p 13 *Pursuit of Happiness*, ©1997 Don Maitz; p 14 buccaneer, Mary Evans Picture Library; p 15 *The Victor and the Spoils*, Howard Pyle; p 16 map of Hispaniola, Edward Weller; p 17 *Closing on a Prize in Heavy Seas*, Howard Pyle; p 18 map of Tortuga, CIA; p 19 *Blood and Thunder*, ©1988 Don Maitz; p 20 Port Royal earthquake, Mary Evans Picture Library; p 21 *Gunner Match*, ©1996 Don Maitz; p 22 (upper right) Khair-ed-Din, Mary Evans Picture Library; p 22 (bottom) Barbary war galleys, Mariners' Museum; p 23 Aruj Barbarossa attacks in galley, Mariners' Museum; p 24 Chinese pirates in junks attack, Corbis; p 25 map of South China Sea, Mariners' Museum; p 26 privateer and British warship, Mariners' Museum; p 27 Mosquito Fleet attacks, Mariners' Museum; p 28 pirates in speedboat, Corbis; p 29 pirates show off weapons, Corbis.

Library of Congress Cataloging-in-Publication Data

Hamilton, John, 1959-
  A history of pirates / John Hamilton.
    p. cm. -- (Pirates)
  Includes index.
  ISBN-13: 978-1-59928-761-4
  ISBN-10: 1-59928-761-7
  1. Pirates--History--Juvenile literature. I. Title.

G535.H25 2007
910.4'5--dc22
                                        2006032014

Contents

The First Pirates

"The Great Mischief and Danger Which Threatens Kingdoms and Commonwealths."
—Charles Johnson, *A General History of the Robberies and Murders Of the most notorious Pyrates* (1724)

The skull-and-crossbones menace of piracy is as old as recorded history. For as long as people have sailed in ships, trading their precious goods across the seas, there have been pirates.

There are many complicated definitions of piracy. To put it simply, as author David Cordingly says in the introduction to his book, *Under the Black Flag*, "A pirate was, and is, someone who robs and plunders on the sea." Pirates don't work for governments; they are not soldiers fighting wars. They follow no rules or laws, other than their own codes. Their goal is to steal, and anyone who gets in their way is fair game for harm, even murder.

Piracy often happens far out on the ocean, beyond the reach of normal law enforcement. It is a crime against all nations. International piracy laws allow any country to seize pirate ships and punish the crew, no matter where they come from. Piracy laws are very harsh; convicted pirates face long jail sentences, or even execution.

Facing page: No Prey, No Pay, by artist Don Maitz.

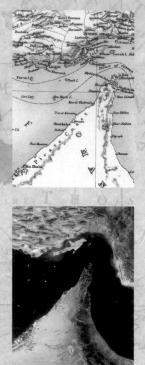

Above, top: An antique map showing the narrow Strait of Hormuz, a place where pirates could easily intercept trade vessels loaded with precious goods.
Above: A satellite image of the same area.

When we think of pirates, we most often think of swashbuckling brigands cruising the tropical waters of the Caribbean Sea. But the Spanish Main was not the first haven for piratical pursuits. Even the ancient Greeks and Romans dealt with the scourge of piracy.

The English word "pirate" comes from a Latin term, *pirata*. That word comes from the Greek *peira*, which means "attack," and "peril." The first sailors were all too familiar with peira. Before compasses and other navigation aids were invented, ships kept well in sight of land. But hugging the coastline made them easy targets for pirates.

As early as 694 B.C., Assyrian King Sennacherib tried to wipe out pirates lurking near the Strait of Hormuz. Middle Eastern trade vessels loaded with gold, spices, and silk passed through the narrow entrance to the Persian Gulf on their way to and from the rich markets of India. Pirates were a constant threat. Unfortunately, King Sennacherib's effort to get rid of the pirate menace was mostly unsuccessful.

Pirates were also very active in the Mediterranean Sea. They liked to prey on Phoenician merchant ships filled with silver and copper from the trading ports at Sidon and Tyre, located on the coast of modern Lebanon.

Another favorite haunt of sea raiders was the Aegean Sea, between Greece and Turkey, with its many islands and hidden coves. Early Greek pirates often raided coastal towns, kidnapping women and holding them for ransom, or selling them into slavery. In 330 B.C., Greek ruler Alexander the Great tried to put an end to piracy. But the threat could never be completely stamped out.

Pirates struck at will throughout the Mediterranean Sea, menacing even the ancient Romans. In 67 B.C., Roman military leader Gnaeus Pompey used a fleet of 270 ships to sweep through the region, attacking every pirate vessel in sight. During a sea battle off the coast of Anatolia, a part of modern Turkey, more than 10,000 pirates were killed, and approximately 400 ships were captured. After Pompey's campaign, which lasted less than one year, the Mediterranean was finally made safe for trade—for the time being.

During the Middle Ages, as civilization expanded, international trade became even more important, especially shipping. Along with the trade vessels, like rats to a ship, came waves of pirates. Beginning in the 8th century and lasting for nearly 300 years, Viking raiders spread terror throughout the British Isles, France, and other parts of Europe. After the Vikings, pirates set sail from nearly every country in the world. Merchant ships were attacked by English pirates, French pirates, and Dutch pirates. Pirates from Asia, Persia, and India terrorized the sea lanes. The world, it seemed, could not escape the scourge of piracy.

Above: Viking raiders land on the coast of France.
Below: A map of the Mediterranean Sea.

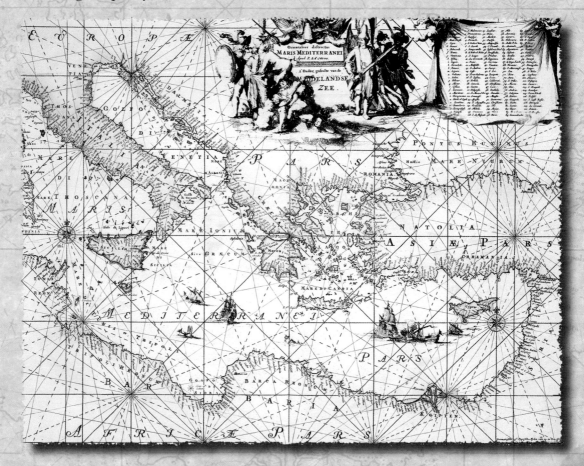

The Spanish Main

Facing page: A Spanish frigate bringing back treasure from the New World— unless pirates catch it first.
Below: Bird's Eye View, by artist Don Maitz.

Pirates terrorized the seas for thousands of years. But when most of us talk about pirates, we think of a very narrow time and place: the Caribbean Sea, also known as the Spanish Main, of the 17th and 18th centuries. This "Golden Age of Piracy" lasted from roughly 1660 until about 1740, a relatively short period of time. Some of the most famous pirates came from the Golden Age: Henry Morgan, Bartholomew "Black Bart" Roberts, Stede Bonnet, and the fearsome Blackbeard. Many pirates made their living preying on galleons, which were large Spanish treasure ships bloated with riches taken from the New World.

Above: A Spanish treasure galleon.
Below: A gold bar recovered from the Spanish shipwreck *Santa Margarita,* which sank near the Marquesas Keys, west of Key West, Florida.

After Columbus made his fateful voyage to the Americas in 1492, Spain and Portugal quickly sent more scouting vessels across the Atlantic Ocean. By 1494, Spain claimed a near monopoly on the new territories. Its navy and its army of ruthless conquistadors eventually controlled almost all of South and Central America, plus the Caribbean.

At first, "Spanish Main" referred only to part of Spain's New World conquest, especially the mainland of Central America and the north coast of South America. But the term eventually included the entire Caribbean basin, plus the Gulf of Mexico. Spain also claimed ownership of North America, but it couldn't keep English, Dutch, and French colonists from settling on the east coast of the continent. Instead, Spain concentrated its efforts on protecting the Spanish Main, and for good reason.

After the conquistadors destroyed the native Aztec and Inca empires, they found a land rich with gold, silver, emeralds, and pearls. Spanish colonists also built plantations. These large ranches, often run by slave labor, produced valuable crops such as sugar, tobacco, and cocoa. Each year, starting in the 1520s, a treasure fleet (or *Flota*) of galleons gathered in various ports and filled their hulls with riches. Then they sailed home to Spain to deposit untold wealth in the national treasury. For more than 200 years, the entire economy of Spain depended on this yearly plunder from the New World.

Spain jealously guarded the empire it had built in the Americas. Some countries, such as England, France, and Holland, tried to establish bases on islands in the Caribbean. These countries were often at war with Spain, and wanted to disrupt the flow of riches coming from the New World colonies. The Spanish, who resented the presence of these trespassers, crushed most of the foreign outposts. But by the 1600s, England successfully built and defended bases on several islands. From these bases, English ships struck against Spanish forces, targeting especially the rich fleet of treasure galleons.

Raiders such as Sir Francis Drake and Sir John Hawkins, who were officially sanctioned, or approved, by the British Crown, became the scourge of the Spanish Main.

National rivalry was not the only reason for plundering Spanish treasure. The vast riches of the New World also attracted pirates motivated purely by greed. Instead of targeting ships in the Mediterranean Sea and northern Europe, many pirates were irresistibly drawn to the warm waters of the Caribbean, where fabulous wealth awaited any crew daring or clever enough to attack the treasure fleets. When sea charts of the region became more readily available in the late 1500s and early 1600s, even more pirates were lured to the Caribbean.

By the mid 1700s, the Spanish treasure fleet system dwindled and then finally came to an end. Enemy raids and unpredictable Atlantic hurricanes had taken their toll. Also, the Spanish had flooded Europe with so much silver that its value plummeted, causing inflation and economic ruin. Ironically, the system that had made Spain rich for more than 200 years eventually caused its decline as a major world power. By 1740, the treasure fleet system was abandoned, marking the end of the Golden Age of Piracy.

Below: An antique map of the Spanish Main.

Privateers

The seemingly limitless resources of the New World created great wealth in Europe. Gold, silver, and precious jewels, plus plantation goods such as sugar and tobacco, were regularly shipped from the Spanish Main across the Atlantic Ocean. Pirate activity naturally shifted to the Caribbean in order to intercept treasure-swollen Spanish galleons.

In the 1600s and 1700s, powerful countries such as England and France issued licenses, called Letters of Marque and Reprisal, which made it legal to attack enemy merchant ships and steal their cargo. Ship captains and their crew who used letters of marque were called privateers. Some of the plunder had to be shared with the home government, but a captured treasure ship meant riches for all, including the crew. The government that issued the letter of marque also benefited because its enemies were attacked without it having to send its own naval ships and men. Letters of marque were a cheap way of increasing a country's armed forces.

A true pirate would steal and rob from anyone, being motivated by pure greed. A privateer, on the other hand, only attacked ships from enemy countries, usually when they were at war. Privateers were sometimes called "gentlemen pirates." Those commissioned by England's Queen Elizabeth I were called Sea Rovers, or Sea Dogs. Sir Henry Morgan, who fought for Great Britain, was one of the most famous privateers of the Spanish Main. To the Spanish, however, privateers were nothing more than pirates. They desperately wanted to see these men captured and executed.

Oftentimes, privateers abused their authority and crossed the line into pure piracy. Convicted pirates were most often put to death, usually by hanging. Many captured cutthroats,

Above: A letter of marque was used by privateers to make their piratical activities "legal."

hoping to escape the gallows, used their letters of marque as an excuse. They claimed they were acting on orders of their home government. Technically, privateer Henry Morgan acted as a pirate when he attacked Panama in 1671, since England and Spain were at peace at the time. In truth, privateers often attacked because of greed and opportunity. When hostilities between warring countries ended, many privateers turned to what they knew best: piracy.

Below: Pursuit of Happiness, by Don Maitz.

Buccaneers

The word "buccaneer" is often used today as another name for pirate. But it wasn't always so. The term was first used in the islands of the Caribbean in the early 17th century. It comes from the French word *boucanier*, a name given to French backwoodsmen of Hispaniola, the mountainous island that today includes the countries of Haiti and the Dominican Republic.

Facing page: The Victor and the Spoils, by Howard Pyle.

Below: A well-armed buccaneer waits to ambush men in a rowboat.

Most of the early buccaneers were French sailors who jumped ship in hope of escaping a harsh life at sea. These deserters fled to the heavily wooded interior of the island. They were rugged outdoorsmen, experts with knives and long-barreled muskets. For food, they hunted the wild pigs and cattle that roamed Hispaniola.

Buccaneers were a rough-and-tumble bunch, used to the hardships of frontier life and the tropical climate of the Caribbean. They cooked and smoked their meat on racks, similar to the kind used by the island's native Arawak Indians. The Arawak had a name for this kind of cooking: *buccan*, which the French changed to *boucan*. A *boucanier* was someone who cooked meat in this way. Later, as English-speaking runaway slaves, sailors, and adventurers joined their ranks, the name was changed to buccaneer.

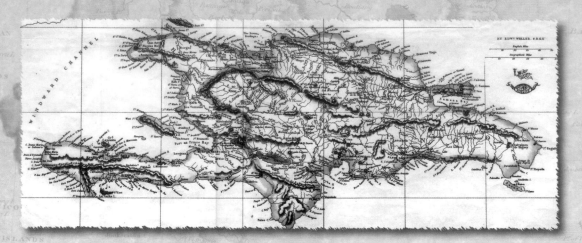

Above: An 1859 map of Hispaniola by Edward Weller.

Most buccaneers hated the Spanish. In the 1620s, many began preying on passing galleons. They preferred sneaking up from behind using small boats, especially at night. The buccaneers could be fierce and cruel. Spanish crews often gave up without a fight, rather than face the wrath of angry buccaneers.

In the 1630s, the Spanish tried to rid Hispaniola of the buccaneers. Most buccaneers turned to piracy. As their numbers increased, they migrated to the north coast of Hispaniola. They also found shelter in the small offshore island of Tortuga.

By the 1650s, buccaneers had formed a group that was loosely known as the "Brethren of the Coast." They followed their own sets of laws. The buccaneers spread out, finding many bases in the hidden coves of the Caribbean islands.

By this time, a majority of buccaneers, especially those in Jamaica, were English. Because England and Spain were at war, the English governors of Jamaica encouraged the buccaneers to continue their raids against the Spanish. The governors gave out letters of marque, which made the attacks "legal."

The most successful buccaneer was Sir Henry Morgan, whose base was Port Royal, Jamaica. Encouraged by the English Crown, Morgan led thousands of French and English buccaneers in raids against Spanish ships and settlements, such as Porto Bello, Cartagena, and Panama.

In 1670, England and Spain finally signed a peace accord, which was called the Treaty of Madrid. Since the two countries were no longer at war, England demanded that the buccaneers stop their raids against passing merchant ships and Spanish treasure galleons. It was the end of privateering. Any buccaneer caught disobeying was branded a pirate and hanged.

Many buccaneers turned to farming to earn a living. Many more continued their piratical ways, plundering ships from new bases in the sheltered islands of the Bahamas. For many years to come, passing merchant ships fell prey to cutthroats. But the age of piracy on the Spanish Main was drawing to a close.

Left: In Howard Pyle's *Closing on a Prize in Heavy Seas*, buccaneers use small boats to sneak up behind a Spanish treasure galleon.

Pirate Havens

Two of the most important pirate bases in the Spanish Main were Tortuga, situated off the coast of Hispaniola, and the Jamaican settlement of Port Royal. From these havens, buccaneers were free to cruise all over the Caribbean, raiding Spanish treasure ships and coastal towns.

The island of Tortuga, which got its name because it looks like a turtle shell, lies off the northwest coast of Hispaniola. (Today the western part of Hispaniola is called Haiti, while the eastern half is occupied by the Dominican Republic.) When the Spanish tried to rid Hispaniola of buccaneers in the 1630s, many found refuge on Tortuga. A heavily armed fortress guarded the island's main harbor. French governors encouraged the buccaneers to settle on the island. The pirates were able to provide better protection from the Spanish than the French navy. The buccaneers also created a lively market for the goods they raided on their piratical expeditions. Tortuga remained a pirate haven until the early 1670s.

Facing page: Blood and Thunder, by Don Maitz.
Below: The island of Tortuga, off the northwest coast of modern-day Haiti.

In 1655, England captured Jamaica from the Spanish. On the southern end of the island was a natural harbor, easily defended against attacks from the sea. The English built up defenses along a narrow peninsula enclosing one side of the harbor, and called it Port Royal.

The English were constantly afraid of Spanish attack. For protection, they lured buccaneers from nearby Tortuga, offering them a safe harbor and a thriving market for stolen goods. Many buccaneer ships made the port their home, which was well situated for launching attacks on the Spanish Main. The English, who felt that a good defense was a good offense, encouraged these attacks.

By the 1660s, profits from the buccaneer raids made Port Royal rich. Henry Morgan, one of the era's most famous buccaneers, made Port Royal his base. It became a lawless city of 6,000 people, a busy port filled with pirates, privateers, cutthroats, and shady investors. A visiting pastor once wrote that Port Royal contained "some of the vilest persons in the whole of the world."

Facing page: Gunner With Match, by Don Maitz.
Below: The pirate haven of Port Royal, Jamaica, is destroyed in 1692 by a giant wave caused by an earthquake.

In the early 1670s, after England and Spain signed peace agreements, the government of Jamaica finally had to act against the pirates. Some were hanged at nearby Gallows Point. After the crackdown, many pirates fled north, finding new bases such as New Providence in the Bahamas, or the sheltered coves of the Carolinas. Port Royal continued to thrive, fueled by the wealth originally brought by the buccaneers.

On June 7, 1692, a colossal earthquake struck southern Jamaica. Port Royal was hit so hard that most of the town slid into the sea, killing more than 2,000 people. Although the town would eventually recover, its days as a pirate haven were finished.

Barbary Pirates

The Spanish Main was by no means the only place to find pirates and cutthroats. Some of the world's most successful pirates sailed in seas thousands of miles from the tropical warmth of the Caribbean.

Above right: Khair-ed-Din, one of the Barbarossa brothers.
Below: Barbary pirates in war galleys attack a group of Spanish ships.

Pirates who cruised the waters of the Mediterranean Sea were called corsairs. Starting in the late 15th century, a powerful group of corsairs emerged who used the north coast of Africa as their base. Called the Barbary pirates, this tightly knit group terrorized the Mediterranean Sea for hundreds of years. The corsairs plundered European trade vessels on the orders of several Muslim countries, which meant they were technically privateers. But to those they attacked, the Barbary corsairs were cutthroat pirates.

Based out of such eastern Mediterranean ports as Algiers, Tunis, and Tripoli, plus smaller ports along the shores of Morocco, Algeria, and Libya, the Barbary pirates used fast and maneuverable war galleys to overtake their victims. These ships used slanted lateen sails to supplement their powerful oars. In the light winds of the Mediterranean, galleys had a big advantage over regular sailing ships.

Some of the most famous Barbary pirates included Uluj Ali, Murat Rais, and the dreaded Barbarossa brothers, who terrorized the Spanish in the early 1500s.

Another powerful group of Barbary pirates called themselves the Knights of Malta. They were a Christian brotherhood that attacked Muslim ships in the 1500s. Their base was a fortress on the island of Malta. They were brutal fighters, feared by all nations. Although they claimed to be holy warriors, they were actually equal-opportunity pirates. Their war galleys often attacked Jewish and Christian targets, as well as Muslim ships. The Venetians—a frequent target of the Knights of Malta—called the brotherhood nothing more than "corsairs parading crosses."

The Knights of Malta continued harassing ships in the Mediterranean Sea until about the 1650s, although they stubbornly held onto their island fortress until 1798.

Below: Aruj Barbarossa, the older of the two Barbarossa brothers, attacks two merchant ships with a small war galley. Seamen and pirates fight with swords and firearms. Archers are also shown on the corsair vessel.

Pirates in Asia

In Asia, pirates were a powerful force for many hundreds of years. There have been recorded accounts of piracy in the South China Sea as early as 589 A.D. Local rulers and warlords along the coast often defied the Chinese government. They set up virtual pirate empires, preying on the maritime trade that flowed through the region in the 13th and 14th centuries.

Chinese pirates used ships called junks. These two- and three-masted sailing vessels, when properly outfitted, were fast and well armed. Pirates liked to capture junks that were used to carry cargo. They easily converted the ships for warfare, cutting ports in the side for cannons, and mounting smaller swivel guns on deck.

One of the most successful pirates in Asia, or anywhere in the world, was a woman called Cheng Yih Sao, or simply Mrs. Cheng. She married a pirate leader in 1801. Together they led a large group of pirates called the Red Flag Fleet, which was part of a confederation of cutthroats who ruled the South China Sea. After her husband died in 1807, Mrs. Cheng took over the family business. At one time, she commanded more than 50,000 pirates. The widow crushed

Below: Chinese pirates in junks attack a trading vessel.

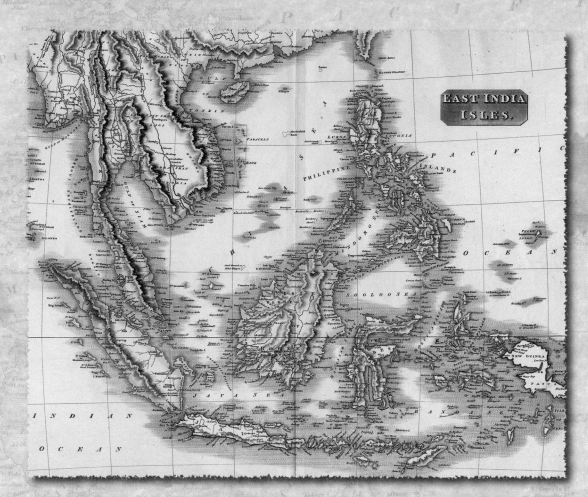

EAST INDIA ISLES.

all attempts by the Chinese government and European navies to stop her piratical raids. She captured hundreds of ships and terrorized villages up and down the coast of the South China Sea, even sending a raiding party up the Pearl River to attack the city of Canton, China.

Knowing that she couldn't escape justice forever, in 1810 Mrs. Cheng accepted an offer of amnesty from the Chinese government. Many of her fellow pirates did the same. Through the use of pardons and aggressive naval patrols, China was finally able to control the pirate gangs. By the 1860s, the Asian pirate menace had come to an end.

After being pardoned for her crimes, Mrs. Cheng, the former pirate leader and terror of the South China Sea, settled down in Canton. She led a peaceful life until her death in 1844.

Above: An antique map of the pirate-infested waters of Indonesia and the South China Sea.

The Pirate Hunters

When the Golden Age of Piracy ended in the early 18th century, the Caribbean Sea and the eastern seaboard of North America became almost free of pirates. But then came the Napoleonic Wars and the War of 1812. Encouraged by American and European governments, privateers once again roamed the waters. When these wars ended, hundreds of privateers suddenly found themselves out of work. They naturally turned to piracy, using such Caribbean islands as Cuba and Puerto Rico as their bases. Galveston, Texas, and Barataria, near New Orleans, Louisiana, were other pirate hot spots.

Above: An American privateer battles a British warship.

Infamous pirates such as Jean Laffitte, Pedro Gibert, and Benito de Soto roamed the seaways, attacking hundreds of American and European commercial ships. Many of the pirates of this age became notorious for their cruelty. They were more than willing to commit murder to cover their tracks. The bloodthirsty Pedro Gibert was once asked by his crew what to do with a group of prisoners. He replied, "Dead cats don't mew!"

Because commercial shipping was so greatly disrupted, the American public demanded that something be done. The United States Navy declared war on the pirates. With help from the British Royal Navy, regular patrols were sent to find and bring the pirates to justice.

Commodore David Porter was a seasoned naval officer, a hero who fought against the Barbary pirates in 1801. In 1823 Porter commanded a group of 16 small vessels known as the Mosquito Fleet. The ships were based in Key West, Florida (then known as Thompson's Island). From this central location Porter struck against the pirates, destroying their ships and devastating their secret bases in Mexico, Cuba, Puerto Rico, and the Florida Keys. Porter and his fleet of pirate hunters killed or captured hundreds of cutthroats.

By 1825, after two years of relentless pursuit by the Mosquito Fleet, the sea lanes were safe once again for commercial shipping. The scourge of piracy in the Caribbean had come to an end.

Below: Small American ships, part of the Mosquito Fleet, right, attack a large vessel used by pirates off the coast of Cuba in 1823.

Modern Pirates

It surprises most people when they discover that pirates exist today. Cutthroats still plunder ships on the high seas, although they look quite different than the buccaneers who terrorized the Spanish Main. Today's pirates are more likely to use AK-47 automatic rifles rather than cutlasses. Instead of sailing schooners and sloops, pirates today use small, high-speed boats to make hit-and-run attacks on their victims.

Throughout history, piracy has always existed where there was a breakdown in local government, where law enforcement was difficult or impossible. And so it remains today. Isolated acts of piracy can occur almost anywhere. But there are certain "hot spots" in the world, lawless areas where unstable governments have little control, where pirates roam free. The South China Sea is notorious for its pirates. The coastal waters of Indonesia, Malaysia, the Philippines, and Borneo can be especially dangerous. Pirates are also active off the coasts of Somalia and Ethiopia, and the ports and waterways of Brazil, including the Amazon River and its many tributaries.

Below: Piracy is still a big problem in the South China Sea. These pirates, from Riau Islands, Indonesia, practice boarding ships with bamboo rods and hooks.

Common targets include passing fishermen, pleasure boaters, or even large cargo ships. The great majority of today's pirates are vicious men who think nothing of covering their crimes by murdering their innocent victims.

One big problem today in stamping out this lawless behavior is deciding who, exactly, is a pirate. The definition of a pirate is someone who robs or murders at sea for private gain. But many pirate attacks today happen in coastal waters, close to land, not far out at sea. And some pirates are actually armed guerrillas who steal from passing ships in order to gain supplies and money for their wars. Other pirates work for local warlords, who run virtual kingdoms beyond the bounds of international law. They are extremely difficult to catch.

When governments decide to crack down, piracy usually decreases. But as long as there is war and lawlessness in the world, there will always be people who go to sea to steal and pillage. There will always be pirates.

Left: Filipino youth belonging to a rebel group show off their assault rifles in Sumisip, a remote village in the mountains of the southern Philippines. Armed pirates, believed to be members of this group, kidnapped 20 people on the tropical resort island of Sipidan off the Borneo coast, on April 24, 2000, taking them out to sea in a boat.

Glossary

Bahamas

A group of islands in the west Atlantic Ocean, southeast of Florida and north of Cuba. Held as a British colony in the 18th and 19th centuries.

Buccaneers

Men who raided and captured ships, especially off the Spanish coasts of America during the 17th and 18th centuries.

Caribbean

The islands and area of the Caribbean Sea, roughly the area between Florida and South and Central America.

Corsair

Another term for pirate. The term usually refers to pirates of the Mediterranean Sea, working off the north coast of Africa. When he was called a corsair, Henry Morgan probably did not like the implication that he was an outlaw, operating without the official sanction of any country.

Cutlass

A short, curved sword having a single sharp edge, often used by seamen.

Frigate

A sailing warship, smaller and faster than a man-of-war, usually used to protect merchant ships or other warships.

Golden Age of Piracy

Roughly the years 1660 to 1740, the era when piracy was at its peak, especially along the coast of colonial America and in the Caribbean. Many former privateers, put out of work as peace spread across Europe, turned to piracy as a lucrative lifestyle. The lack of a strong, central colonial government led to ineffective and scattershot protection of ships at sea, at a time when many vessels carried valuables across the Atlantic Ocean.

Grappling Hook

A hook with multiple prongs that is attached to a rope, designed to be thrown some distance to take hold of a target. Grappling hooks were used in naval warfare to ensnare the rigging or hull of an enemy ship so that it could be drawn in and boarded.

Letter of Marque

Official government document granting a ship captain permission to use his personal armed vessel for capturing and raiding ships of another country. Used by governments to expand their naval forces at a time of war.

Man-of-War

A large sailing warship armed with many cannons. These ships were used on the front line of a battle.

Pirates

Rugged outlaw seamen who capture and raid ships at sea to seize their cargo and other valuables.

Privateers

A ship, or its captain and crew, operating under a letter of marque. A country issued letters of marque to permit the raiding of ships from specified countries that it had engaged in war. The captain and crew were paid out of any booty they took from the ships they attacked. Also known as "gentlemen pirates."

Schooner

A two-masted sailing ship, easily maneuverable and able to navigate shallow waters.

Sloop

A fast sailing vessel with a single mast. Outfitted for war, a sloop had a single gun deck with 10 to 18 cannons.

Index